PRASAD R BATTU

THE MOST UNDERRATED DEPARTMENT HUMAN RESOURCE

Contents

Preface

The entire book that I drew up and edited as per the human resource experience I have. It may vary from ones experience to mine.

I never thought of writing a non - fictional book since publishing my first fictional book 'Love Can Happen Multiple Times,' but one day unexpectedly an idea struck in my mind to write a book on Human Resources, how it is misunderstood and made fun in the company when it actually supports all sorts of employees and employers.

And then I started to write it down to the points that many misunderstood the department and continued to expand on.

All the hard work to complete this book is to erase workers' misunderstood image of the HR. The HR department sacrifices a lot of things and won't get proper respect and rewards where it works for the respect and rewards of every employee.

Thank you for purchasing this book, and hope that respect for the HR fraternity will increase with this.

Acknowledgement

The sites below helped me get the necessary data and do some research on the HR content.
I wish to thank every contributor to the pages. It was very supported by the data to complete this book.

blog.hrps.org

quora.com

Google.com

www.proformative.com

www.inc.com

hbr.org

www.thebalancecareers.com

www.betterteam.com

www.hr.com

cite.hr

www.peoplematters.in

www.lucidchart.com

www.ere.net

www.pwc.com

HR = YOU CAN MAKE FUN OF IT

Because,

Everyone says HR does nothing and roams around the office corridor and cafeterias. HR is the most underrated department in any entire organisation.

So what does HR actually do?

There is a huge difference between a balanced human resources department that contributes to the organisation's growth and a remote HR that resides somewhere in the basement archives and only pops up for the company holiday party once a year.

Here's a detailed description of what the HR department is doing (or what they should be doing) to meet employee needs. To ensure that your company has an excellent HR department, see to it that these recommendations are met.

What is an HR department?

The HR (Human Resources) department is a group that is responsible for managing the employee life cycle (i.e. recruiting, hiring, onboarding , training and firing employees) and administering employee benefits in the simplest possible terms.

What does human resources do?

Ask any employee what an HR department is and you will get a response that deals primarily with the most unpleasant aspects of work: HR violations, layoffs and firing. But the fact is there are human resources for employees to help. For humans it is quite literally a resource.

Here are some of the tasks that your Human Resources department is busy doing every day.

1. Recruits you

HR needs to understand the needs of the organisation and ensure they meet those needs when recruiting for new positions. It's not as easy as simply throwing an ad on Indeed: you'll need to analyse the market, communicate with stakeholders and manage budgets.

Then, once the role is advertised, more research is needed to ensure that the right candidates are attracted and brought forward. Recruitment is a massive and expensive business; the right candidate can revitalise a whole company, but the wrong candidate can upend operations.

2. Hire the right employees

Human resources are responsible for arranging interviews, coordinating the hiring efforts and embarking on new staff. They are also responsible for ensuring that all the paperwork involved in hiring someone is filled out and ensuring that everything is successfully navigated from the first day until each following day.

3. Process payroll

One of the main human resource elements is payroll processing which involves the timely and accurate processing of the salaries of each of the employees working in the company. This offers all other incentives and bonuses to the employee's salary, along with tax deductions, leaves and any other deductions. Operating as an HR, the specialist will be required to check the employees' working hours, pay each employee's monthly payments on time, figure out the tax and insurance deduction, set up new staff

2

members, measure all types of time, submit tax forms, and handle special situations such as sickness leaves and maternity leaves.

4. Conduct disciplinary actions

This role may be the reason why HR appears to get a bad rap. Disciplinary actions can lead to the loss of a valuable employee when navigated inappropriately, and can even result in litigation or poor reputation. But disciplinary action can result in an employee's performance if taken appropriately.

For example, if a company discovers a particular employee is routinely late and continues to be late even after multiple warnings have been issued by the employee, HR may step in and investigate the reason for the lateness. It may be an opportunity to extend benefits such as employee counselling or offer additional resources to help the employee learn to be on time. Rather than paying the cost of firing, and then hiring a substitute for that employee, it could be a learning opportunity that could enhance the career of that employee.

On the other hand, disciplinary action often isn't the right course to take and a staff member should be let go. Departments with the best human resources know when an individual is not the right fit for a company and would be happier somewhere else. Sometimes, it's in the best interest of the employee to be let go, as painful as it seems at the moment. To establish a team's cohesiveness and wellbeing, it is up to HR to develop a strong enough relationship with managers and employees alike.

5. Update policies

Policies must be revised or at least reviewed annually as the organisation changes. It is the job of HR to make official policy updates and suggest policy changes when they no longer serve the firm or the employees. A policy can sometimes be updated

3

as a response to an event. HR should always be included in these decisions, and consult with them.

6. Maintain employee records

The maintenance of HR records is mandated by law. These records help employers identify skill gaps to assist with the hiring process as well as analyze demographic data and comply with regulations. They also provide personal details for each employee, and emergency contacts.

7. Conduct benefit analysis

Staying competitive is important when attempting to attract the best talent. When the benefits are more enticing, a potential candidate may choose another organisation with lower pay. HR must review related organisations on a regular basis to see if their benefits are compatible. For example, your company may consider including Employee Parents insurance in its benefits list (because let's be real: Health of Parents can have a big impact on your employees' happiness).

How does HR support employees?

HR has fewer objective functions in addition to the seven instances above, which are mostly organisational responsibilities: it exists to help employees thrive.

Workers are after all the biggest single asset to any company. It follows, then, that it is of utmost importance to protect their safety. Here are four ways HR helps support employees' emotional and job needs:

1. Providing career growth

Stagnation is bad for business and having the best employees with the company is wise. HR can provide career paths to help guide each employee into a long corporate future. HR may then periodically check in to guide employees further on their career paths.

2. Offering continuing education

The aforementioned career growth sometimes requires further training. The company can provide educational assistance, and HR will help to determine which courses and training programs are best suited to an employee on their career path. HR can also work with managers to make sure the work schedule for the employee is flexible enough to allow the employee to attend classes.

3. Training and supporting managers

They're not born bosses, they 're made. HR will help managers with management guidance, ensuring organisation and staff are as stable and efficient as possible. This can include sending managers to formal training and retreats regularly.

4. Supporting health and wellness

It's important to remember people are workers. They will need assistance weathering mental illness, health problems, mortgages, births, childbirth, and a myriad of events in life. HR will help support employees in any of these cases and in any other.

When to contact Human Resources

A human resources department that never interacts with staff is not doing their job. When you develop an onboarding process, remind new employees about when to reach out to HR and what resources HR has to provide. The HR department should schedule regular one-on-one interviews with employees to check in on their career progression, comfort in their roles, and any other issues that the employee may have.

In these and similar situations, employees should feel comfortable reaching out to their HR departments in light of these responsibilities:

- When you or a colleague are abused or discriminated against by your superiors, including your boss
- When you have concerns about benefits, including health insurance provided by the company or rights guaranteed by law
- When your personal circumstances change e.g. having a child, any issues with the Shifts
- If you have concerns about advancing at the company, including opportunities to shadow other employees or take part in further training
- When you need a specific third party to work on a work - related problem

Building the best HR department

The department of human resources contributes heavily to the culture of a company: if HR is harmful, workers will be depressed and less likely to seek support from HR, either with job or personal issues.

Nonetheless, if HR is sincerely concerned about employee well-being, then the atmosphere will be one of transparency and development.

HR = SHOE RACK

Yeah, you read it correctly. HR is compared to a Shoe Rack in front of a temple. Which can only be used while going in and coming out. Thus, at the time of joining and before leaving the organisation, employees think they only needed the HR department.

There are many things HR does as mentioned previously, apart from only taking joining and taking exit interviews.
But why only employees like them on the first day of joining?
Only because of the HR who handled his recruitment process, the employee joins that organisation.

If the new joiner seems too anxious, then HR takes care of him by offering something to drink or eat to make them comfortable.

HR will obviously not want to make them more uncomfortable by offering something they may not want before they go ahead and make the preparations.

HR will take them out and show them around the office campus for a little stroll. They tell them about every building's past and initiation, how it was before they entered, or how it used to be like it was a few months or years ago.

HR helps them familiarise themselves with the surroundings with little interesting stories so the walk isn't getting too boring.

HR Introduces them to their co-workers and other team

7

members.

HR will explain the new employee, and acquaint them with the culture of the company.

Why don't employees mess with HR and speak to them on the Last Day of Leaving with extra coated sugar?

HR will hold his final payment cheque if an employee messes up.

HR will share the negative feedback in the call to background verification.

In his statutory payments, HR will bother employees.

When leaving an organisation an employee would assume that if they mess up with them, HR will stop all his emoluments. But the truth is that no HR will intentionally stop any payment to workers but if there is any serious reason, they will.

No HR spoils the career of employees by giving negative feedback in the background verification process. But if the problem is real, they 're not even going to let the employer suffer by recruiting a bad employee. So decide for yourself: Are you a bad or a good resource?

Whether joining or exiting, HR processes are the same. At the time of hiring, they are strict, but in a happy mood of joining a new company, the employee will ignore the process, but once they join the organisation, they feel that HR is a burden because they ask about their attendance, time records, and records of leave that annoy all the employees.

He is very stringent when taking exit formalities as before when the recruiting starts, but now the employee will note the stuff because HR procedures are a waste of time for the employees. But HR is the same and he does his job.

HR = NOT COST TO THE COMPANY

The HR department was viewed primarily as an expenditure that in the past was not explicitly generating revenue. Back then, HR had to justify their budgetary needs to the company. Since then things have changed dramatically. Today, the budget for HR is given. Management has come to understand the importance of managing human resources and its overall interest in improving productivity for companies. HR is not considered a cost centre any more now. In fact, its role has evolved into one of a profit centre where it now makes strategic decisions which drive the growth and profit of the company.

Here are three key factors driving this shift:
Realising that everything is about people:

No matter what the business is, a business needs people. Human capital is the guiding force behind any company to make profit. A company is basically non-existent without the enthusiastic workers working for the right job. HR plays an important role in maintaining positive employee engagement.

Practices such as helping new employees adapt, celebrating high performers and training low performers are some of the ways in which HR has helped improve the company's effectiveness. HR provides an opportunity for the company to search out new business opportunities and increase its sales by doing all of this and more.

Knowing a well-developed staff member is a profitable employee:

It is just as good a company as its workers. Therefore, employee development is crucial to the growth and productivity of the company. There are different positive outcomes for the different types of employee training. For instance, in-service training programs may lead to better customer service for a hospitality business.

Another form of seminars, leadership and management, will help employees develop and move up inside an organisation , resulting in time and money saved from looking outside. Training in the ever-evolving IT technology provides employees with the knowledge and ability to remain at the top of the industry, resulting in improved productivity and increased revenues.

An organisation that does not believe in education and growing its workers runs the long term risk of losing out. Education not only increases morale and productivity, it also places the company well within the market, which contributes to competitiveness and in effect attracts people of higher quality. While direct managers of a company's human resources, HR plays a vital role by keeping employees actively involved by strategic learning programmes. A company with exposure to the very best talent enjoys the benefits of direct impact on profits and growth from industry. This generation of income comes from human capital being handled innovatively.

Recognising the transformation and influence of HR in the substance of a company:

Transformation of Human Resources is coming. Organisations are moving towards lean manpower. This is basically a situation with a smaller core workforce supported by a larger remote or virtual workforce. Technology has created new ways for employees to work and to contribute to the content of the company.

As technology leads us toward a re-imagined workforce, HR will be a key player in managing this transformation successfully to ensure continued growth and profitability for an organisation. HR helps generate value with a technology-receptive and social-ready attitude by raising business costs while at the same time hiring the right talent to produce profit for the organisation. HR now holds a critical seat at the management table, rather than being seen as a cost of doing business, one that directly influences the profitability of any business.

HR = ONLY GAMES

" It's a play that makes people unafraid to fail and confident to try new things. It's a play that helps us do serious things better because we enjoy them and feel a sense of joy in our achievements."
— Jake Orlowitz, Head of the Wikipedia Library, Wikimedia Foundation

Gaming is an integral part of our life, starting from infancy. Even our education system has an extra class of extra curricular activities that includes games in it. It's not rare to find adults interested in playing games on their smartphones! Tapping this innate desire for sports, corporate HR departments have also chosen to use Gamification to inculcate this phenomenon into their management – the latest buzz in the HR domain. With research indicating that only one in ten employees is *'engaged'* in their jobs and the remaining employees are *'not engaged'* or *'actively disengaged,'* many companies turn to Gamification to actively engage their employees.

Gamification is described by the Gartner Group a global research and advisory firm as: The use of game thinking and game mechanics in non - game scenarios such as business environment and processes, specifically in recruitment, training and development, and motivation to engage users and solve problems.

Gamification can be a real game changer by enhancing employee engagement and making the work process more exciting and enjoyable for employees.

Many companies, such as Deloitte, Cognizant, etc., turn to gaming to improve the skills of the workforce, solve different problems and bring in new talent.

Here are the various kinds of gamification of HR!

Gamification can be divided into two categories according to Karl Kapp professor of instructional technology at Bloomsburg University. One is structural gamification which requires the addition of gaming elements to existing content to help people move through it; the features could include points, badges, leaderboards, etc.

The second form, gamification based on content, transforms the content itself into forms of a game, but with business goals at its centre. These are called 'violent' games too.

How does gamification work in HR and favour the organisation?

Gamification takes advantage of people's natural competitive nature to motivate them to perform better. It helps employees better engage in the company, wards off malaise and provides a fun-filled entertaining atmosphere that allows employees to intensively tackle their obstacles. It also enhances group effort and cohesion.

"Gamification is 75% psychology and 25% technology" – Gabe Zichermann

Well, the answer depends on how well that's done. A gamified solution which is poorly designed will not succeed. Therefore one needs to be specific about the objectives and what sort of action is expected as the desired result.

The primary aim of introducing workplace gamification is to promote a particular type of company-friendly behaviour. And for the actual behaviour to occur, Professor B.J. Fogg, a Stanford University experimental psychologist, says three things must converge at the same time: viz, motivation, ability and trigger. Tools for gamification succeed when they:

- Motivate employees to do a particular activity (chance of winning rewards, recognition of fame, incentives, etc.). For example, HR teams may reward employees internally by offering 'Referrer Bonus' badges, motivating employees to refer top candidates and playing an active role in the acquisition of talent thus assisting the HR department. Instead of the game mechanics, emphasis must be on motivation.
- Make it easier for employees to perform a task by splitting them into considerable chunks according to their ability.
- To complete the tasks, boost or trigger their competitive attitude. For example, mundane tasks such as participating in a compliance training program will have little takers to fill out forms such as expense sheets, benefit form, etc.. When these are made attractive by providing credit to individuals performing these tasks by monetary incentives, this will generate demand and workers will come forward to perform these tasks on a voluntary basis.

Gamification, when it meets the above motivation, ability,

and trigger factors, will definitely help to achieve the desired behaviour and provide the benefits required.

Prerequisites For A Good HR Game!

Here are the various factors characterising good HR gameplay.

1. Facility of easy access through platforms

Gamification should be easily accessible via multiple devices. Employees should be able to access gamified tools whenever they quickly get free time, and it should also be compatible across multiple devices so they can use whatever device they've got in hand at the time. Gamification helps to easily learn and train in a business if used correctly.

2. Cater to the interests of the employees

Know what motivates your workers, and set up gaming systems and strategies in line with employee interests. For example, profile badges that acknowledge contributions from employees may be the motivating factors for technically interested employees, and hence such badges may be used in game building.

3. Meet The Strategic Objectives

Gamification will cement the business strategy of the company. Investment in gamification apps should be made in key areas such as on-boarding, training, etc. to help achieve the strategic goals of the company accordingly.

4. Have A Clear Gamified Objective

What goal is to be accomplished through the established game needs to be clear. In order to get a proper return on investment, the concept has to be clear. For example, before applying PwC, required prospective employees to have a clear understanding of the company.

Traditionally those prospects have surfed in their company website career page for less than 15 minutes to learn about the company. The result was a game called Multipoly that allows applicants to test their ability to work in PwC. As teams, members work together to solve real - world problems and projects that PwC has undertaken, such as construction acumen and digital skills. The result was an increase of 190 percent in prospective candidates and more than 70 percent interested in learning more about working with PwC.

True to what Bill Roberts says' Game mechanics can't be sprayed on ice cream learning programs like nuts. 'One has to be clear about the goals for the game to succeed.

5. Conduct Proper Analysis

All game data should be thoroughly analysed to better under-stand the workers and know what inspired them and learn about their behaviour.

Customised tools and applications for gamification of corpo-rate human resources

Different flexible and personalised tools such as eMee, MindTickle, etc. support organisations in HR and Gamification.

A global communication consulting firm, Ketchum uses an app called LaunchPad to gamify its junior - level recruitment process, primarily for its Summer Fellows programme. For its 10 week internship programme, the company receives more than 2000 applications for 15 positions. To avoid the tedious process of passing through all applications, it uses an interactive game via Launchpad where applicants not only play against a bot but also get other gamers' responses commented and voted on and earn points. There are two challenges in the game, and it is open for two weeks and can be done on a mobile device. Gamers earn 10 points for their challenge or comments any time another participant votes. Afterwards, top gamers are selected for the interview stage.

Today different gamification tools are available to suit multiple HR areas. Whatever the company's goals, there are many applications that can provide a response. Below is a list of different software that helps with diverse aspects of HR functions:

- Cuckootech: Time and attendance a gamifying application.
- Employee connect: An engaging program to improve communication between the employees
- Badgeville: A robust system for keeping employee paperwork, reviews, overtime work etc.
- Hyphen: A real - time, mobile employee engagement platform.
- Axonify: It is a micro-learning gaming platform.
- Bunchball: It puts together behavioural economics, big data and approaches to gamification. Bunchball Nitro was the first technology platform to integrate game mechanics into digital experiences other than game play.
- Mambo.IO: Mambo. IO provides on - site and cloud - based gamification software.
- Spinify: For gamification it's the customised leaderboard platform. It is a solution based on TV and the desktop.
- Moroku: It is a web - based gamification solution suited for small and medium enterprises. It is integrated with practices of mobile banking and payment, and also supports mobile gaming and social media.

How gamification works to improve productivity of HR!
Here are some of the Gamification applications in HR areas and related success stories!
1. HR Gamification In Recruitment Potentials
Company : Marriott Group of Hotels

Mission: To encourage Millennials to apply outside the US for vacancies

Gamified Solution: Hotel Marriott 's international chain has developed a *'My Marriott'* game in which players play the role of managers in a virtual hotel kitchen and deal with the issues of hospitality and perform virtual hotel tasks. The players earn points and receive rewards. This lets the applicants get an idea of the work in which they would be interested, and also helps the company remove those applicants who lack the necessary aptitude.

This game was developed primarily to multiply Marriott's recruitment in global arenas outside the US and encourage more millennials to participate. This gamification is an excellent example of attracting and better engaging potential hires around the globe, and also giving them a bird's eye view of what the job would be like.

Result:The company was able to gain a better understanding of the job by potential recruits before they decided to work for the company, thereby ensuring easy on-boarding later.

Few more examples

For those in the technology stream, NP Paribas bank used two online games, one a coding game, and the other in finance with virtual bankers and finance-interested clients.

The global accounting firm KPMG has run a game called '80 days' for potential recruits. This was an adventure game involving players flying the longest time on a hot air balloon to meet various en - route challenges. Depending on such competitive games the potential recruits could be identified.

2. Gamification In HR Onboarding

Gamification helps in the fun - filled way in quick embarking of new employees. Many businesses have begun using onboard gamification.

HCL Technologies sends an interactive game to those who have received job offers approximately 30 days prior to their start to embark on them, check their commitment and also predict the rejections of the offer.

ExxonMobil's Employee Orientation Program uses Scavify (An interactive app and employee engagement platform and other HR solutions) to welcome new recruits and enable them to explore the campus, learn about the company's culture and interact with colleagues on a fun - filled journey.

3. Gamification In HR Training And Development

Company : Deloitte

Mission: Make senior executives addicted and engaging in a leadership training programme

Gamified Solution: Deloitte Leadership Academy used the gaming app from Badgeville to give training on learning , knowledge sharing and brand value creation. Deloitte designed a leadership-training program for its senior executives but was having trouble getting them involved. Deloitte took Badgeville's help to use elements such as badges, leaderboards, and status symbols that assessed employee participation and training course completion.

Result: The result was a 50 percent reduction in the time taken to complete the training program and an increase of 46.6 percent in the number of employees returning regularly to the site to complete the programme.

HR Gaming Boosts Performance And Learning

Gamification is also used to improve learning and ultimately to boost performance.

Company : Microsoft

Mission: Agent Learning and communication across the globe. Gamified Solution: Using gamification, Microsoft's Consumer Support Services improves agent performance and learning. Gamification has been introduced to improve agent performance by incentives, improved on-the-job learning and to motivate employees at the call centre as well.

Result:It was able to pass on knowledge across its scattered base of agents and also motivate communication across its base of agents.

Company : Walmart

Mission: Make use of short games to improve safety training Gamified Solution: Walmart used gamification techniques to provide its scattered workforce of more than 5000 partners across its various distribution centres with safety training. The gamifying platform used various gamified applications of three minutes, which were integrated into the workflow of the employee.

Result: This resulted in a 54 percent decrease in mishaps and also became a massive hit among employees who began discussing not only the games but also the importance of following safety protocols.

Gamification In Employee Engagement And Collaboration

Company : Qualcomm

Mission: Employee Engagement.

Gamified Solution: Qualcomm has introduced simple gamification techniques for its internal Q&A program over the stackoverflow.com platform, where workers ask various technical questions and anyone can answer them. Employees receive bonus points for, and they receive ratings and votes for best answers. Furthermore, there are special awards for best performers such as the Archaeologist to answer questions that have been unanswered for about 30 days. The employee is also remembered in the form of an insignia depicted in their profile.

Result: There were fewer unanswered questions and better engagement with the employees.

Company : Google

Mission: Making employees submit information on travel expenses routinely and on time.

Gamified Solution: Google employees get an allowance for every role when they go on a work trip. Google gamified this process by making workers who had an unspent allowance choose to use the remaining money with three options: to combine it with their next pay check, to save for future trips or to lend to a charity of their choice.

Result: Compliance was 100 percent when travel information was submitted within six months of the game's launch.

Future Trends

In the future, gamification will occupy a prominent place among HR tools, allowing employees to balance work pressure with the creative medium. If the right gamification is played, employees are bound to get involved well. While gamification is gaining popularity among large organisations, the bandwagon will soon be joined by small and medium - sized businesses too.

Gamification is not only a game but a HR game changer. Are you prepared to go ahead in your search for inspiration and change the game rules?

HR = DISTRIBUTING SWEETS

There's a joke cracked on HR's all the time that they'll just be distributing sweets on Diwali and running rangoli competition among employees other than they have no work to do.

Yeah. HR distributes sweets since joy is to be shared with all, and conducts rangoli competitions to add a few more colours to the work life of all employees and improve their spirit.

Diwali is without a doubt the most important festival held in India. Celebrating the festival at the workplace has emerged as one of the best strategies for employee engagement.

Rituals are just as important to organisations as they are to families. And, nothing is more important than the annual rituals that companies create around the seasonal holiday celebration. Celebrating festivals at work has become one of the most important initiatives of employee engagement. Such celebrations not only bring together employees but also help create a more inclusive atmosphere across departments and boost employee morale, promote employee engagement, and encourage team spirit and joy. Today, organisations have taken on new and innovative ways to celebrate the festival.

Decorations:

You must have heard the saying, 'May the light of the Diwali lamps fill your life with success, happiness and joy.' Traditionally, we celebrate this festival of lights by lighting up beautiful clay lamps every year. Today the overall Diwali decoration concept has changed over the years. Earlier, on-the-job decorations meant rangolis, roses, electric lights, etc. Today's decorations, however, include LED lights, lamps, electrical diyas, flowers, rangolis, paper lanterns, paintings and wall designs etc. Everything is protected from the exits of the alleyway to the workstations.

It is common for businesses to turn their entire workplace with creative new ideas to decorate their office, with workers sometimes involved. For instance, workstations have been renamed at Ernst & Young to resemble landmarks from the Hindu epic Ramayana. Times of India went eco - friendly and decorated their office with streamers of paper cups and with shredded papers on Rangoli.

Few companies will reward the workers who creatively decorate their desk or workstation with a theme.

HR can ask their employees to come to office in a traditional attire to feel different, colourful and fresh on the auspicious day, instead of the usual formals.

Shrinking bonuses and bloating coupons:

The big fat bonus that had previously taken care of an EMI or helped plan an expensive purchase is now being replaced by gift vouchers and coupons. According to a study from ASSOCHAM Social Development Foundation, an online survey was conducted to gage the opinions of 1,000 full - time office workers and about 500 human resources professionals on Diwali festival bonuses and gifts they desired. The result of the survey showed that some 45 percent of office workers wanted cash or gift vouchers. According to the same report, however, HR professionals reported that cash rewards have the lowest impact and do little to boost satisfaction and performance among employees.

Beyond Sweets and Dry Fruits:

Gifts are one of the reasons why diwali is one of the workplace festivities to be anticipated. Corporate gifting has become a tradition in which colleagues and staff show gratitude, affection and create goodwill. Gifting a box of dried fruit and sweets has been a thing of the past. Deciding employee gifts is one of the hard situations in which to be. Before you give employees a present that they like, there are certain things to consider. Even if you manage to zero down on the kind of gift you want to give, you still need to get the best in the category, quality, and price.

Companies are turning to a variety of new ideas these days, including luxury watches, technology gadgets, crockery, designer apparel, expensive souvenir pens, home decoration, movie tickets, free holiday packages, and gift hamper essential for festive seasons including torans, diyas, aromatic candles, etc..

The competitive world is pursuing new gift ideas, but few businesses are still distributing 'Soan Papdi' to the workers who are cracking their heads to whom to move the package. And it was viral on social media with the same memes.

Celebrations at work:

Today companies have a series of events lined up to engage the employee at work.

It goes without saying that they cultivate team spirits by organising enjoyable Diwali events at the workplace. Many organisations take on innovative activities to foster a sense of camaraderie, and team spirit that includes volunteering, potluck lunch, flash mob, selfie competition, Fashion Show, Desk Decoration, etc.

Needless to say, HR plays a vital role in ensuring that all the activities take place during the celebration as per schedule, such as coordinating the squad, approving the budgets and forming a core team to execute things promptly. Nevertheless, one of an HR's most critical responsibilities in organising every organisational event is to get the work done when the workers are in a festive mood. Another critical element in celebrating a festival at the workplace is addressing inclusion. An HR has to make sure that no one is excluded as a result of the festivities. The decorations, activities and presents should not make people of different cultures or religions left out of the festivities.

HR = NOT FOOTBALL TO THE BOSSES

"You know one person is your boss, and you know you will get a lot of requests from another person. And you have to do your best to accommodate them."

–Matthew Bidwell

Sometimes, almost everyone finds it tough to keep the boss happy. But what if you had a steady stream of overlapping requests and opposing deadlines coming from two or more managers simultaneously? There are increasing numbers of workers reporting to multiple bosses, experts say, and working out how to control those who oversee you comes with their own specific set of demands and opportunities.

Dual reporting was an old technology implemented in the 1970s, created to address the problem of leaders and workers who need to work beyond their vertical, siloed relationships in reporting. Such relationships appear on the chart of the company, but in short, it is a map of who reports to whom, who has authority over whom.

The problem with this vertically oriented management technology is that there is no way people can work across silo boundaries. Technically, if you wanted to work with someone in another department, you would have to go up the chain of command until you met a specific supervisor, and then scale back down before you found the person you wanted to work with.

This was far too cumbersome, and so a new idea came into being. What if you could report someone in another silo to your vertical or functional leader and also someone who might be a business partner or an internal customer?

For example, I could have two bosses, my HR leader as well as an Operations leader if I reported to HR but was placed at another location where there was a project for the Operations group.

This neat, new invention of dual reporting was also known as Matrix Management. Which the reporting structure will be explained through direct lines and dotted lines.

Lets understand these two terms at the centre of this issue :

Direct (Solid-Line) Reporting : Solid-line reporting describes an employee's relationship with his relevant manager. The supervisor provides the employee with primary direction, manages the main financial resources on which the employee depends in carrying out his job, performs performance reviews with the subordinate and provides all other direct supervision.

Indirect (Dotted-Line) Reporting : Dotted-line reporting describes a relationship between an employee and a secondary manager which provides the employee with additional oversight and guidance when performing his work. The aim of the dotted-line relationship is to ensure that the dotted-line manager has the authority to give the employee some level of influence and leadership. The dotted-line manager shall provide the solid-line manager with input regarding the performance of the employee for inclusion in the annual performance review of the employee.

The difference between the dotted line and the direct line fads. People have to fight to ask who your boss is, it's not as easy to answer anymore. You're going to have different bosses, the one involved in a particular project, but that individual may not be the one actually doing your performance review, so you've got different bosses you're trying to please. Knowing whom to keep happy, making clear where loyalties are, facilitating communication, all these hurdles multiply exponentially with two or more bosses. Not only that, but you often handle managers' demands that aren't talking to each other, and there's a lot of ambiguity, a lot of people thinking you're their top priority. Everybody wants a piece of you so conflict management becomes a big challenge. Much of that is about how boundaries are treated. Because you can get totally overwhelmed if you are not careful.

In a dual-reporting scenario, major problems occur when the decisions taken by the various managers are in dispute. Most times, the managers are in constant conflict with each other, and when one wants more attention, there is no mediator in the middle. Thus the employee is stuck in the middle, being constantly pulled in various directions. These situations are common in dual reporting structures, and do not serve the organisation's overall goals.

Working for more than one manager presents numerous challenges. There are three main issues which the employee will face, however:

1. Overloading : One of the biggest risks with more than one person assigning you to work is simply having too much to do. If you report to multiple bosses who oversee your efforts on various tasks and projects, it's too easy for each boss to treat you as if you don't have any other responsibilities.

2. Conflicting messages: The more bosses that you get the more conflicting messages you receive, this often happens out of ignorance, your bosses don't know what the others are saying or because people push their own agendas. Different bosses often have different expectations and what impresses one could mislead another.

3. Loyalty : Some bosses want to know that they're your first priority. If you have more than one boss who feels this way, it's easy to get caught in the middle. Reporting to more than one person often requires you negotiate between competing demands for your loyalty.

Principles to Remember
Do:

· Seek out the most common challenges of having multiple bosses so you can handle them proactively
· Keep a positive attitude and remember that the conflicts are most likely due to the situation and not because of you
· Find out which of your managers will take the decisions that affect your career

Don't:

· Try to speak to each other on behalf of one boss try to get

them to talk to each other, if possible
- Keep a work and task list hidden from any of the managers
- Push for transparency if it not rewarded by your organisation

HR FIRST, THEN EMPLOYEE FOLLOWS THEM

From time to time, we are all late; it's a part of life. We've all been there from being delayed in traffic, breaking down cars and even sleeping through an alarm! But from my viewpoint, the saying HR should get to the office first so that workers stick to the timing is incorrect. Because if an organisation has 4000 workers on the same campus and it has different floors, no one can manually monitor their time even if the HR enters the office way before all employees, hence the organisations have implemented a biometric tracking system.

But as an HR, both the efficiency and the overall success are important to punctual workers who are positive and enthusiastic. Employee lateness is one of the most common problems that business owners and managers find impacting on the company's effectiveness. Although managers assume that employees are sometimes late, if employees start to be late on a regular basis for work, actions need to be taken to protect the company and improve the team's work ethic.

As an HR, you expect staff members to be late sometimes. However, managers and employers can not accept a situation where an employee is constantly late for work, simply because this acceptance will only aggravate the situation and worsen it.

If you notice a staff member arriving late persistently, that should be dealt with accordingly. Otherwise, the employee in question may think this is not a problem and start turning up even more late. In addition, the actions of the late employee may even cause other staff members to consider why they are bothering to arrive at work on time , leading to other late employees.

And there might not be an end to the problem. Showing approval of the constant lateness of an employee may cause them to become more compliant with other company policies, and you may find that the team's overall quality of work and work ethics is declining.

Managers pay their staff for their time at the end of the day, and they are asking staff to work specific hours to ensure all the work can be completed. An employee who is constantly late therefore effectively steals time from the company. A late employee can start falling back on their job and either hurry stuff, or leave them unfinished. Furthermore, persistent lateness of employees can cause tension among colleagues, as team members who work alongside them may end up having to do more work to cover up for their colleague causing some resentment and ill-feeling. Teams work best when working closely together and communicating well so the team's overall effectiveness can be compromised.

Dealing with employee lateness:

There are no tough and swift rules to deal with someone who is always late. Every HR is different, just as every employee and their personal situation is different. Nevertheless, with that being said, if you want to deal with a late employee, there are certain steps you should take.

Document the rules

A policy on lateness could be considered excessive by itself, but a section on lateness could be inserted into existing policies and procedures covering absence management or time and attendance;

For example, The policy should include:

Employees' standard expected: details of working hours, emphasising that employees should be ready and prepared to start work as soon as their shift is scheduled to begin.

The procedure for reporting lateness: If an employee knows that they will be late, to whom will they report that?

Information of how to track and record your working time: do you use timesheets or do employees need to physically clock in when on-site?

Provide information as to how workers can make up the time they have missed on arriving late, if necessary.

A report on the future disciplinary action that may be taken for repeated lateness.

A comment which should be avoided late as it is disruptive for everyone.

Ensure that any new policies or changes to the process are communicated to all staff and equally enforced across the entire company. If this is something new for your business or if you have a particular problem with lateness of employees, then consider running brief seminars for employees to attend to highlight the impact of lateness, go through the processes with them and give them the opportunity to ask questions.

Maintain records

Keep track of employee lateness and remember that if you see one or two employee members being much more late than the rest of the work team, you may need to deal with them.

Keeping records ensures that when you talk to the employee in question you will be able to use them as evidence, showing them information rather than expressing your opinion about their tardiness.

Proactively deal with the persistently late employee

Do not wait until you're angry and annoyed or the rest of the team feel upset. Before you get to this level, talk to the late employee to help prevent it from getting to that point. Schedule a meeting with the employee concerned and, in the meantime, collect all the information you have about their working hours, incidents of lateness and reasons etc.

Respect their privacy

While it is important that you broach the subject with an employee who is always late, be aware of their privacy. Take them to one side to address their lateness instead of questioning them and voice your concerns at the headquarters, which may cause embarrassment.

There may be a sensitive or personal explanation for their lateness, so approach the discussion with respect and give them the opportunity to take your concerns into consideration and say their piece.

Reward improvements

It should be strengthened to acknowledge altered or enhanced habits, no matter how minor. Rather than penalising the employee, make a point of remembering their steps to correct their lateness. Your employee will know why they're constantly late, so in principle they should know how to fix them.

Trying to remain calm when meeting the late employee, do not make it personal and stop getting angry. Speak about their lateness via your questions, provide them with evidence and refer back to employee lateness policy in your business. Explain that you want to understand what's triggering their lateness, and find out if you can help with something.

Try to understand if they are late if you have any personal problems, medical problems or other reasons. Remember to take into account any possible issues that could arise from prejudice and any changes that the organisation might reasonably make to help the employee.

HR = NOT A TERMINATOR

When an employer has made a job offer and the prospective employee has accepted it, both sides start optimistically, expecting what each feels will be a successful new partnership of work. We know of course that not all relationships with the work are successful. A variety of factors may prevent a task arrangement from working: the employee may have overestimated their skills or may have engaged in inappropriate behaviour, the employer may have understated the difficulty of the job, or business needs may require a reduction in the number of employees.

There is the simple fact that the termination of an employee sometimes is necessary. It's a dirty job but it's got to do someone. The termination of an employee is one of the most difficult tasks to be performed by an HR, and neither time nor experience makes it easier. And it's a highly charged emotional problem for the HR, employee, the supervisor and the rest of the staff.

Employees who are not on the line of fire can feel 'survivor's guilt' because their colleague in a tough economy has been terminated. While thinking along those lines is both legitimate and compelling, remembering that non - productive and/or insubordinate employees have a long - term negative effect on productivity and morality is extremely important. Often, an employer has no choice but to fire.

Most employers have placed policies and procedures that detail the correct disciplinary measures and termination steps. Written policies and procedures provide managers with guidance on how to handle the delicate issues of disciplinary action and termination at work as they arise. The presence of written policies and procedures also ensures some degree of continuity and equity when action on employment is required.

Anyone with the authority to discipline and terminate an employee should not only recognise the policies and procedures but also be held responsible for following the appropriate protocol. While some managers may not bother learning, understanding, or following the procedures, the workers do. A person in authority who does not understand or follow the policies set out leaves the door open to a lawsuit.

In the absence of established policies and procedures, managers will have no official guidance on how to discipline and terminate workers, which may contribute to contradictions in how these two actions are handled. One of the simplest charges to bring is an accusation of discrimination against an employee in a protected class. If management ignores company policy, a court may find an inappropriate reason for the action. If an employer does not have a set protocol or if the manager fails to follow it, a court may look at how the employer has in the past handled similar situations with other employees and make their judgment by establishing that behaviour as the unwritten policy of the employer.

Once all the considerations have been weighed, and termination has been determined as the only option, you need to take time to prepare for the end meeting. Specific factors must be discussed and coordinated with the relevant parties before any closing meeting can take place. The HR will have to make arrangements regarding:

- Contractual obligations owed to the employee or from him
- Benefit issues – all forms and notices should be provided
- The return of the property of the company and how it will be done
- Collecting personal property of the employee at the office
- How will the employee react to termination? In anticipation of that reaction, appropriate arrangements should be made
- Where the termination meeting is to be held? public places should be avoided so as not to cause the employer or employee embarrassment
- Who will be present during the meeting? conclusions should be observed by another management member or Human Resources
- What will be discussed at the meeting, and what should be kept clear, succinct and consistent
- All documents— if you offer a severance package in return for a dismissal of claims, an attorney may draft the agreement. An poorly written release may have no legal force, and may be used in front of a jury against the employer.

What they say is true: Honesty is the best policy. Do not sugarcoat or play down the reasons; doing so will come back to haunt you. Often, the alleged misconduct of a disgruntled employee toward employers is critical to a lawsuit for wrongful termination or discrimination. If an employer fails to address these issues in the termination meeting or worse, makes statements inconsistent with the true reason for termination, it can damage the case of an employer in the judge's and jury's eyes.

Credibility is the key when tackling discrimination or retaliation issues. To that end, be mindful of the following when you're ready to terminate an employee:

- Remind the employee that several opportunities for improvement have been provided and that the desired progress has not occurred.
- Provide realistic examples of poor performance. Do not overdo it; rather, stick to what can be proven.
- Don't let the meeting turn into an argument or a debate.
- Treat the employee courteously, and do not embarrass him or her publicly.

It does not require immediate wage payment at the time of termination; however, some companies have specific rules on timely final wage payment.

Paying all the money due at the time of termination could deter some disgruntled employees from submitting a claim. After all, being fired is stressful enough. It's never an easy decision to terminate an employee, but the steps you take to prepare for that day can make things as easy as possible for all involved parties.

Here, HR plays an emotional and dirty central role. According to the cost cutting call from the management, or an employee whose performance does not match the organisational requirements must be terminated. Thus only HR will speak to the person and communicate after a thorough discussion and understanding of the reality. It's their job responsibility and part of their job but they also feel bad as a human being before trying it.

HR = NOT A DATA ANALYST

Data analytics can not be managed by the business partner who handles the HR operations. He can do the basic analysis but with the analytics tools they can't handle the whole bunch of data because they are more people managers than data.

Difference between an HR data analyst and HR business partner The work of the analyst is primarily focused on data collection, analysis and reporting, the business partner (BP) is more involved in communication with line managers and helps to solve their HR related problems. In practice, the BP relies on soft skills for 90 percent, while the analyst relies on harder (data) skills, if not more, than on soft skills.

This means the HR BP is an internal consultant who helps the manager achieve business goals. This work is sometimes very operational, sometimes more tactical but it is very much applied to the business. The HR analyst steps in if the BP and the manager run into issues that can be solved using data.

The role of HR analyst is usually only relevant in larger firms and classified as an entry level position. A successful HR analyst has great interpersonal skills and is strong at communicating as well as being a good problem solver and able to work with data. Works closely with the HR director and across the entire function.

What does an HR analyst do?

HR analysts are responsible for identifying and assisting with the resolution of HR related problems, ensuring that they adhere to the policies and objectives of organisations. It is all part of the role to analyse and evaluate data and reports, feed the results back to the relevant managers and advise on changes and improvements.

The job involves creating and delivering business wide presentations and training, when required. Good communication skills are key, as you will build relationships with employees at all levels and in some instances liaise with partners or clients.

HR analyst responsibilities

- Identify and work with the HR team to resolve various human resources issues
- Communicating with customers as needed and assisting with troubleshooting and any business needs of clients
- Help with job audits and human resources investigations and follow up with relevant parties
- Creation and distribution of expert presentations and training on HR related topics throughout the business
- Providing advice and support to numerous organisational departments on human resources policies , processes and best practices
- Analyse and present data and reports to the appropriate field of expertise, identify errors and advise on solutions
- Assist the HR team in advancing and moderating operational policies , guidelines and systems to foster best practice within the company

- Reviewing and inputting employee and candidate data into relevant HR databases
- Potential supervision with training and coverage and feedback on performance of the employees

What does an HR Business Partner do?
The HR Business Partner (HRBP) is responsible for aligning business goals with staff and management in designated units of business. The position formulates relationships across the HR function to provide value - added service to managers and employees that reflect the organisation's business objectives. The HRBP maintains an efficient level of business literacy regarding the financial status of the business unit, its midrange plans, its culture and its competition.

HRBP Responsibilities

- Carries out weekly meetings with their respective business units.
- Consults with line management, providing HR guidance when appropriate
- Analyses patterns and metrics to develop solutions, plans, and policies in collaboration with the HR group
- Manages and resolves complex issues relating to employee relations. Conducts investigations which are effective, thorough and objective.
- Maintains in-depth knowledge of the legal requirements relevant to day-to-day employee management, raising legal risks and ensuring compliance with regulations
- Provides day-to-day performance management guidance to line management (e.g. coaching, counselling, career

development, disciplinary actions).
- Works closely with management and staff to improve working relationships , build morale, and enhance productivity and retainment.
- Provides HR policy guidance and interpretation.
- Develops terms and conditions for new hires, promotions and transfers.
- Assists international staff with expatriate assignments and related human resources matters.
- Provides guidance and feedback on the restructuring of business units, workforce planning and the preparing of successions.
- Identifies the training needs for business units and the coaching needs for individual executives.
- To assure success, participate in the evaluation and monitoring of training programs. Follow -ups to ensure that training goals are met.
- Carries out other duties related as assigned.

HR = NOT A RECRUITER

HR has a broader scope of work and a small part of it is recruiting. And now, a few individual organisations have separated recruitment from HR, and it is treated as a separate dimension. But few organisations will extend the choice of recruiting to the HR and they will not know that recruitment will not be included in the core HR activities.

Try to understand the recruiting industry, then.

Recruiting, now widely referred to as talent acquisition, has and continues to evolve sufficiently to make the recruitment industry truly create its own environment, not a living being in someone else's universe.

Through order-taking and administration to training and consulting, recruitment means business has become a value - added service to any organisation , regardless of size or sector.

The days of help-wanted ads are gone, with the typewritten or fax resume answering. Receiving piles of paper resumes and covering letters where the practice was to break them into A-B -C stacks with written notes on suitability; then converting the volumes of paper with electronic notes into a simple searchable database wasn't that long ago. The first-level reporting was provided by using a simple chart to count how many resumes received, reviewed, accepted, interviewed and hired. Headhunters relied on placing candidates by their Rolodex.

Today ATS (Applicant Tracking System) is the heavily invested tool companies that rely on for recruitment and reporting activities. In other words, welcome Big Brother, the sluggish, process driven, and time consuming support. Some are better than others; however, the ATS' purpose isn't necessarily to make the position of the recruiter easier, more efficient, or more competitive. It is designed to pull reports from the supervisors and allow candidates to have an online experience. Candidates are often receiving feedback that their resume is sent to a 'black hole,' and when they receive an electronic response to accept or reject their application, there is no personal contact and trust in the company in which they are seeking employment. The *'accessible, candidate oriented'* system lacks the two way human interaction. The reports are often fraught with the potential risk that data integrity is low. For the recruiter, it's not unlike the previous method of A-B-C piles to read any resume obtained and to decide yes to screen or reject, or perhaps.

Job boards dominated the market, offering the candidate access to multi industry job listings in one easy place. Over time, employers were offered the opportunity not only to market their hiring needs but also their job brand. Today, organisations are relying on their corporate website and places like LinkedIn to accomplish the same goal. Job search engines such as Naukri and Indeed encourage candidates to search other websites for employers in hopes of finding new jobs.

RPO (Recruitment Process Outsourcing) has hit the market and many industries have tried this outsourcing model and most of the companies applied it. Vendor management systems are bridging the relationship between agencies or headhunters and their business customers.

Once heavily relied on testing and evaluation centres and today online psychometric testing is being used to assess the fitness of a candidate. *'Which animal are you?'* Sort of interview questions have been popular and we're used to the sequence of behavioural interview questions lately.

Social media, social networking, and online interviews are now helping to build constructive and interactive communication with applicants, recruit top talent, and improve one's job brand. Mobile technology provides better means to improve communication with candidates in both ways.

Sourcing has (and is still) become a critical skill for the recruiters. With Google's existence and Internet access, Boolean search strings have developed into a hot commodity. Innovative ways of producing or headhunting top talent are an art form today. Professional networking organisations opened doors to engage as a recruiter and network activities to find the next best candidate. LinkedIn brought this idea tenfold to the next point, and today many recruiters are using this technical social media website as their principal hunting ground.

LinkedIn Recruiter offers a solution for managing pools of talent. CRM (Candidate Relationship Management) is the latest recruitment trend, taking advantage of software marketing professionals that have been using it for years. Whatever program is applied, there is no doubt that technology has contributed by proactively developing talent pipelines to meet critical recruitment needs.

Recently there has been a debate as to whether recruiting, which is actually a human resources feature, should come under marketing. Many agree recruitment should work as their own entity. Although there is interest among other key stakeholders in partnership with HR and marketing, we as talent acquisition professionals provide our hiring managers, senior leaders and CEOs with a unique and indispensable service.

Recruiters have also grown in the way they interact with hiring managers and senior leaders. Recruiters have once been an order-taker and more recently have worked with managers to identify their hiring needs, perform panel interviews, evaluate candidates and conclude the contract, i.e. recruit the applicant selected. Today, the recruiter is a right hand partner in many cases, providing advice and guidance not only on the hiring process but also on the job market, the strength of the internal and external candidate pools and trends in industry. Analytics and possible solutions to key problems come with the results. Recruiters are getting better at this every day as an industry of professional talent acquisition experts. The emergence of '*big data*' and metrics helps identify critical talent, provides us with a more strategic source, and provides intelligence on how the competition is performing in hiring talent.

My questions are: Why don't they mention their own role? Why can't they drop down menus to their own listing in the job board? These are lumped together under human resources. HR has a significant place in an organisation and some of its structure can be extended to hiring; however, attracting talent is an art of its own, not a weakness for a human resources position. Most organisations understand this, and have a distinct leadership and team structure to help recruit and acquire new talent from their company. They are called recruiters and not professional human resources. Yes, they are not professional human resources. It's time for the next stage of evolution. It's time to highlight HR function as a key contributor, noteworthy as we are already and isolate the recruitment function from HR.

HR = NOT A SALES JOB

As explained in before chapters that HR means not Recruiting, it is just a part of human resource. And recruitment is a sales job where a recruiter attracts the applicant to apply for the vacant position by providing the details of job and company profile.

HR and hiring are two skill sets which are very different.

There is some overlap in some organisations, but there are some very good recruiters who in HR are terrible and some people in the HR who would be terrible recruiters.

Human resource department consists of those people who manage the employees of the company , and make different policies for the betterment of the organisational communication among the company. Who makes different plans to make the environment of the company more favourable for work, they discuss how they can improve the efficiency of employees. They also recruit people for their company.They are basically one of the key parts of a company without which company can't work effectively.

HR deals with issues like on-boarding, compliance, dealing with employee complaints, payroll, training and development, audits, liaising, exit formalities, etc.,

HR = NO RESPECT

The HR job is like a police job charged to protect a company, where you can't ask for anything in return, at least respect.

What HR Does?

They scrutinise you.
   Judge you and decide your future at the company.
   They tell you what all you can do in the workplace and what can't be done.
   What to wear, how much to wear and in some cases, what NOT to wear etc.
   HR departments are respected, revered and regarded as an essential part of the organisation, in many organisations. They are however found hated and unnecessary in some.
   Most employees hate HR, because they don't want to be monitored, performance checked, and excellence measured. Such people refuse to understand that HR has a job to do, and processes and regulations will be in place to comply and adhere to ensure that the organisation keeps it healthy and does not become free for everyone. Sadly, most of those people are all under-performers, and when they reach leadership positions, they do not command respect from their juniors.

Now the RIGHT reasons for hating HR: One, I do not hesitate to say that a vast majority of Indian HR folks are simply not only incompetent, and have not seriously attended to the real science and art of their craft, they are also generally, the biggest showbaaz, and flippant of all other types of professionals. Somehow, they believe that what makes HR effective is deceit, planning, gaming and sophistry.

This approach makes them really practice HR in a crooked manner, sometimes putting people off the wrong way. That's how and why they are loathsome to the other staff, who don't really have much time to engage in all this except for some innocent gossip, nor are they capable of thinking so cryptically.

Management generally expects the HR department not to have a voice of its own. In many organisations the HR department is regarded as the company's only voice and this has nothing to do with the size, and everything to do with the culture and mindset of the CEO. These departments are not permitted to have their own voice, they are not supposed to give their opinion, to partner with the business and to provide sustainable human solutions.

Basically, they are to only deliver the decision already taken by someone else who is a business expert, but not have any understanding of human resources. And if he has a good understanding, this decision has not been made together, and some knowledge behind the decision making has not likely been communicated with the HRs, which is where the HR team can not provide a great solution, and bungled with the final output.

Strong HR professionals gravitate gradually towards industries that are required to have a broad aspect of business cooperation from HR, where joint decision making is taken and the rationale for each decision is understood.

If you hate the HR department, it means your management

doesn't believe in having an empowered HR team and most likely it's because management is dictatorial in Its own style.

Now who enjoys to hate HR, Let them.

HR simply implements policies that have been developed for the greater good, and yes, every program could be built on, but so what? Where is Your share of the company's fun and entitlement?

When you break rules, the police separate you from society, HR separates you from your workplace and your job.

HR is an ungrateful job.

Whatever an HR would do to you, in the space of days you would forget.

HR didn't give you that vacation you wanted?

HR could accommodate you to the best of their abilities, but you just can't like them.

They are your favourite people to hate, because you have to take out your crappy work frustration on somebody!

Still, HR's know they have no respect for their job but they're not going to compromise on their work.

HR = CAN'T TAKE LEAVES

If HR takes leave by mistake then the entire office starts to poke and talk about it, as if HR got a company sponsored international trip.

HR will not even have the right to take his own leaves. Because they are required to complete tasks according to the timelines and deadlines. By chance they complete all tasks on time and request a leave then his functional manager approves it and the operational manager disapproves and vise-versa, because the manager needs to go on vacation. When there is no manager in the office then HR must and should be available, and there is no chance of taking a leave when the manager is in the office.

Boss is always right. They never agree to approve the leave application of HR. But they do go on foreign trips without fail every time.

If an HR takes a day's leave, the total work will get stuck, but if managers go for a week or more, there will still be work completed because that's how our organisational structure benefited managers. They have subordinates, who take care of their work when they are on holiday. But for us we don't have subordinates and every responsibility for HR is unique to every individual and we can't ask our peers to complete our tasks whenever we're on leave because they're already overloaded.

HR only prepares the letter of offer and appointment where the details of the leaves are mentioned in the big letters but can't claim those leaves for themselves.

If HR requests leave, it is a crime and the manager says that HR needs to understand the rules, and should always be in office. The manager will not approve leave. If HR asks for a leave, the manager thinks it is an argument and imposes a disciplinary action.

So the policies that HR explains to all the employees will not apply to them, like that managers will change the policies that will benefit them much more.

Every time on the leaves HR's compromise and the leaves will be lapsed. Because HR must please their managers and accept their orders, or else they will be thrown out of the organisation.

By chance if they authorise leave, HR needs to work on the laptop at home because managers need some urgent papers whenever HR is on leave and they will work on those reports at home. It is better pack the bag and go back to the office.

HR = A REGULAR EMPLOYEE LIKE YOU

Like any other department, HR also has a job role and responsibility to handle the staff, and a collection of rules and regulations derived from management.

HR is a unique department dealing with people having emotions and feelings. Understand machinery is easier to handle than humans.

As how your KRA's are going to be checked, likewise HR's KRA's will also be tested and the reason you dislike HR is because of their KRA that they need to complete the task without fail.

HR knows employees are making fun of them and their department but they just ignore it and work for betterment of employees.

Employees treat HR as a Shoe Rack, but they still enjoy being a shoe rack that employees can use.

Management will give the HR department less importance, yet they sacrifice it and again begins to work to improve an organisation.

HR does not only make employees work, but also play, and distributes happiness in the form of sweets.

HR gets squeezed in between two managers. They can not complain to anyone if they assign tasks which can not be included in their assessment.

HR never makes any employee termination decisions, it's a management call or a self - made error by an employee that leads to termination.

HR does not come from any parallel universe but is a normal person who bridges the relationship between an employee and the management. Their jobs must be valued and their contributions rewarded. Do not underestimate them as they will not generate any income for the organisation, and do not treat them as an unnecessary burden.

They are the real reason for getting the right workforce at the right place at the right time. No hiring of the right talent, i.e. no income, no success and no organisation without them.

RESPECT HUMAN RESOURCE